ALL ABOUT BLACKJACK

John Gollehon

D1173286

A PERIGEE BOOK

Perigee Books
are published by
The Putnam Publishing Group
200 Madison Avenue
New York, NY 10016

First Perigee Edition 1988

ISBN 0-399-51461-9

Printed in the United States of America
4   5   6   7   8   9   10

CONTENTS

ALL
ABOUT
BLACKJACK

CHAPTER 1

BLACKJACK, HOW TO LEARN THE GAME

The number of potential players who would like to play blackjack, or other table games for that matter, is staggering. And the casinos know it. In recent years, most forward-thinking casinos have instituted "learning" sessions for these potential players, taught right in the casino, on the very tables. The casino "schools" are scheduled frequently, sometimes every day; and with little exception, the classes are usually jammed.

It seems almost sacrilegious to learn how to beat the casino, *from the casino!* Do you really think that's the best way to learn . . . and win? True, the sessions are free, but you get what you pay for.

A great number of these potential players are actually players already, but what do you suppose they play? Slots! That's right, slots. Because no one has to be taught how to pull the arm, or how to read the simple instructions, or how to listen for the jackpot. Pull the arm, and if you win, coins drop. If you lose, it's quiet. That simple.

And that expensive! Slots are no way to really challenge the casino. The odds are heavily stacked against you. Sometimes the casino has a 10% advantage (or more!) going for it. Forget slots, unless "entertainment" is all you're looking for.

THE BEST GAME IN THE CASINO

Hopefully, *All About Blackjack* will help you progress to a much better game, with far better chances to win. What about the other table games you ask? Well, Craps and Baccarat pose some interesting short-term possibilities, but over the long term, a relatively small casino advantage will eventually get your money. Like slots, Keno and Roulette are almost sure losers. Again, the casino has a solid, high percentage going for it at these games, based on purely random probabilities. Skill is no factor.

Indeed, blackjack is the right game to learn. At least you chose the right book! But what's the best way to learn? What will it take to give you the confidence to walk up to a table?

PLAYER RELUCTANCE

This question brings to mind another problem, other than simple instruction, that the casinos have been trying to solve for decades. Player "reluctance." The casinos will gladly teach you how to play, and so will I, and many other authors for that matter. But there seems to be a certain "intimidation" associated with table games, especially craps and baccarat, that prevent a lot of players from making their first wager.

Casino studies have shown that an unusually high percentage of women and senior citizens simply resist playing. While Dad plays blackjack, Mom plays the slots. The assumption is that some people fear embarrassment by making a silly mistake, or simply showing their inexperience in front of other players who may be watching. Sadly, they're missing out on the best part of the casino, if indeed they have the desire to gamble at all.

To my way of thinking, the hesitancy to play is merely a lacking of confidence. Besides teaching you how to play, *All About Blackjack* makes special effort to give you the confidence to play, based on skill. Hopefully, this text will give you

what is so often lacking in the multitude of players
. . . **confidence, discipline, and desire to win!**

Incidentally, the worst possible way to learn
blackjack is from a friend. Unless, of course, your
friend is an expert player. There are very few. And
then again, just about everyone thinks they're an
expert!

KNOWING HOW TO PLAY ISN'T ENOUGH

In 1983, I wrote a best-selling book on casino
games, titled *Pay the Line*. I included data on *both*
craps and blackjack, and designed the book for
both the beginner and advanced player. No easy
task!

In short order, I found out that the truly inexperienced player wants a purely basic, entry-level text
to begin with, void of any unnecessary mathematics
and sophisticated strategies. But blackjack is a complex game! Can we condense and simplify the instruction without short-changing the reader?

Absolutely! Since much of *Pay the Line* had been
written ever so carefully for the beginner, I've in-
corporated some of that material in this book. The
sections that might tend to confuse the reader have
been dropped, or carefully rewritten.

Learning the basic game rules and basic strategy
for all the player options is obviously essential, but
it simply isn't enough for a good player. I've included light material on card counting, that many

authors ignore at the beginner's level, but frankly must be discussed, even in elementary terms. *Without at least a rudimentary knowledge of tracking cards, the player's skill is seriously compromised.*

Equally important, some attention must be given to the player's discipline at the tables. Without the discipline to quit winners, to play at the right time, and to look for the best opportunities, all other strategies become virtually useless.

All About Blackjack presents what I think is the best possible introduction to the game—usage of material that has already been widely accepted and acclaimed, in a new, easy-to-understand, step-by-step format.

I can't guarantee that you'll win. No one can. There will always be an element of risk. With that understanding, let's get started.

CHAPTER 2

THE BASIC GAME

Blackjack is played with a standard deck of 52 playing cards, in fact the same "Bee" brand that you can buy in any drug store, made by the U.S. Playing Card Co. Jokers are removed.

You and any other players at your table (up to 7) are playing against the casino, represented by a dealer who merely deals the cards, and has no other "interest" in the game. The dealer's actions are mandatory, based on strict game rules. Technically, the game could be dealt by a machine or a monkey, since no playing skill is required.

The only possible "skill" to worry about is cheating, but frankly, it happens very rarely, if ever, especially at the larger, well-known casinos. Twenty years ago, perhaps. But today, with the priceless value of a gaming license, and the casino's ability to generate substantial income honestly, cheating is an inconceivable enemy.

Cards are dealt from a shoe (a box containing more than one deck) or by hand to the player and the dealer, each getting two cards. One of the dealer's cards is face-up for everyone to see, while the other is face-down.

OBJECT OF THE GAME

The simple object of the game is for the player to have a hand that totals "21" or is closer to 21 than the dealer's hand.

The "number" cards count as face-value, the "picture" cards count as 10, and the "ace" is counted as either 1 or 11, whichever is better to make or approach 21. *The four suits have no significance in blackjack;* only the number value is used. For example, a 6-value card and a Queen count as 16; two Queens count as 20.

If the player is not satisfied with his first two cards, he may ask for an additional card, or as many as he likes until he "stands" (is finished). If the player takes too many cards and exceeds 21, it's an automatic "bust," and the player immediately loses. Toss your cards on the table between the betting area and the dealer, indicating the bust. The dealer will remove your wager. In some cases, all the player's cards are dealt face-up; you never need to touch the cards, and shouldn't. In this case, when you bust, the dealer will remove your cards (and your wager) for you.

When all players at the table have acted on their hand, the dealer turns over the card dealt face-down (hole-card) and stands only if the total is 17 or more. The dealer is required to draw cards until the hand totals at least 17 or more. If the dealer "busts" in the process, all players who did not "bust" themselves are automatic and immediate winners.

If however, the dealer does not bust and has a hand that totals between 17 and 21 (which it must, because the dealer draws to make at least 17, and more than 21 is a bust) the hand is compared to the player's to see which is closer to 21. Whichever is closer, wins. If both the player and the dealer have the same total, it's called a "push" (a tie) and there's no decision on the bet. In that case, the player is free to remove the wager, increase it, or decrease it. Only after a push, or after a win, can the player again touch the chips in his betting area. Never touch your bet after a game has begun. Casino personnel are very suspicious.

Now, read this brief section again carefully until you fully understand it. It's the essence of the game! If you're wondering on what hand-totals to draw cards, or at what point to stop drawing, don't worry about it now. We'll cover that later, at precisely the right time, for all possible hand combinations.

BLACKJACK PAYS 3 TO 2

All bets that win are paid at 1 to 1 odds, "even money." If you bet $5, you win $5, and so on. However, if the player's first two cards are a 10-value card and an ace, it's called a "Blackjack" (wins outright) and is paid at 3 to 2 odds. You'll receive $15 to your $10 bet. *The 10-value card does not need to be a picture-card.* A "ten" of spades or any other suit is worth just as much as a Jack, Queen, or King. Any 10-value card and an ace make a Blackjack.

If the dealer receives a Blackjack on the first two cards, the player loses at even money (only the amount of their wager) unless the player also has a Blackjack, in which case it's a push.

INSURANCE

The only other exception to the even money wagers is called "Insurance." Here's how it works. If the dealer's upcard is an ace, the dealer will ask all the players if they wish to take insurance. To do that, you bet an additional amount up to one-half of your original wager, betting that the dealer does in fact have a 10-card underneath, in which case you win 2 to 1 for your side-bet. The dealer always "peeks" at the hole card if an ace is showing to determine if he has a Blackjack, before the players are given the option of taking more cards.

In most casinos, the dealer also checks the hole-card if a 10-value card is showing, again to determine if the dealer has a Blackjack.

Today however, many casinos no longer allow "peeking" at the hole card (unless an ace is showing) to discourage collusion between the dealer and a player, attempting to cheat the casino. It's possible a dealer could "signal" the hole-card value to a player and thereby give the player a tremendous advantage.

The bottom line on insurance is *don't do it!* It's a silly bet that only increases the house percentage.

HIT OR STAND MOTIONS

To recap, the most important option the player has is to either "hit" or "stand." Your way of indicating to the dealer that you wish to hit or stand depends on whether the cards are dealt face-up or face-down. Some casinos deal all the player's cards face-up, other casinos deal the player's first two cards face-down.

Cards Dealt Face-Up

At tables where the cards are dealt face-up, the player never needs to touch the cards. To signal a hit, the player may do either of two motions.

I prefer to point at the cards, actually touching the table with my finger about two to three inches from the cards. This way, there's no question that I want another card. Unfortunately, some casinos frown on this action for whatever illogical reason.

The other motion is to simply bring your hand toward you in a scooping motion. But be sure you do this over the table, so the "eye in the sky" can see it to record. (The casino's video-tape cameras are there to protect both the casino and the player. Don't be intimidated by them. Every table is in fine focus.)

If you don't want another card, I recommend that you simply put out your hand, towards the dealer, as if to indicate "stop." The casino recommends a horizontal motion as if you're wiping a piece of glass above the table.

However, it's been my experience that the latter motion can easily be confused with the opposite signal, especially if the player is particularly sloppy with his motions. Try my way.

Cards Dealt Face-Down

At tables where the cards are dealt face-down, you obviously must pick up the cards to read your hand. If you do not want another card, simply place both cards face-down on the table and slightly under your bet. In most casinos it's all right to simply place the cards within close proximity of your wager.

If you want a hit, keep the cards in your hand until it's your turn to play. Then, lightly "scrape" the card edges on the table, towards you.

Incidentally, it makes no difference whether the cards are dealt face-down or face-up in blackjack. This ain't poker! But, it does make a significant difference to card-counting that we'll discuss later.

SPLITTING

Another important option for the player is to "split" identical cards in your original hand, such as a pair of 8's. When this option is available, the player does not just automatically do it! The decision to split or not to split your pair depends on whether or not it will be an advantage to you.

When we get to our "basic strategy" later in this book we'll detail each possible pair combination in comparison to the dealer's up-card, and make the decisions for you.

For now, however, let's prematurely make two important rules abundantly clear: **Never, never, never split 10-value cards, such as two face-cards, and never split 5's. Always split aces and 8's!** If you're an inexperienced player, see if you can quickly understand the solid reasoning behind these two important rules.*

When you wish to split your cards at a face-down table, simply position your cards face-up and behind your bet (to the dealer's side). Then, make another wager of the same size and place it directly *beside* (not on top of) your original bet. At a face-up table, you only need to make a new bet inside the betting circle to indicate the split, since your cards are already in position.

The dealer will know that you are splitting the pair, and will give you two more cards, one to each card you split, in effect establishing two new hands that are working for you. If you receive another identical card, you may split again, and you'll have three hands in play.

Splitting Aces

However, all casinos do not allow the re-splitting of aces. To make matters worse, after the dealer has given one card to each of the split aces, the hands stand. The casino will not afford you the option of hitting. Regardless, splitting aces is still a strong player advantage. Always do it.

---

*Splitting 10-value cards is my favorite example of greed. You're throwing away an excellent hand! Players who split a 20 should have their head examined.

DOUBLE DOWN

Here's an option that figures significantly in the player's ability to adjust the percentages. You may "double down" on your first two cards by making an additional bet up to the amount of your original wager and receive *only one card* from the dealer. One hit.

Obviously, the time to double your bet is when you have a hand-total of 10 or 11 and the dealer's up-card is 6 or less. That's the ideal situation. Another 10-value card will give you a 20 or 21. Even an 8 or 9 will give you a pat hand (17 or better). That's the reason we told you earlier never to split 5's. The two 5-value cards give you a hand-total of 10, and that's usually a good time to double down.

We'll give you the complete basic strategy for doubling down, and all the other player options, later in this book. You'll know exactly when to do it, and when not to.

As I've mentioned before, the casino industry has been negligent in their efforts to standardize game rules. Perhaps it's an element of competition that shouldn't be standardized. Whatever, the rules do vary, and doubling down is a good example.

Some casinos limit double down to only 10 or 11. Still other casinos will allow double down on *any two cards,* and that's a big advantage to the player, as you'll learn later.

Unfortunately, most casinos not only have different rules, they *change* their rules about as often as your gas bill goes up. So the best solution is to simply ask before you play.

SURRENDER

"Surrender" is an option that few players understand or readily use. Probably because most casinos, until recently, did not offer it or promote it. Now, as blackjack players become more sophisticated and discriminating, casinos are turning to it more and more.

Eventually, it's estimated that virtually all casinos will have to incorporate it, in order to stay competitive with the casino "across the street."

This is what it means to the player. If you don't like your first two cards, and that happens a lot, you can "surrender" the hand and lose only one-half of your bet. To enforce surrender, simply state "surrender" to the dealer, and throw in your cards. The dealer will remove half of your bet and you're out of the woods. It's that simple.

I refuse to play blackjack in any casino without surrender rules. I don't want to hit a 15 or 16 against the dealer's 10. The only time surrender is not allowed is when a dealer has a blackjack. So wait for the dealer to peek when an ace or 10-value card is up. If the dealer does not have a blackjack, you're allowed to surrender.

A SOFT HAND

Any hand that includes an ace has two values . . . a soft value and a hard value. If our hand is an ace-6, the soft value is 17, the hard value is 7.

Although it doesn't come up that often, there's a decision to make whether or not to hit a soft 17, 18, or 19. Usually, a soft 20 is good enough and the player stands. But it's important to remember that *a soft-17 will not bust*. A 10-value card will simply make the soft-17 hard. Depending on the dealer's up-card, we actually may want to double down on a soft 17, if the casino allows it. We'll give you the basic strategy for soft hands in the following pages.

Dealer May Hit Soft 17

Earlier in this chapter, I told you that the dealer is required to draw to 16 and stand on 17. That's the basic rule on the "strip" in Las Vegas but in Northern Nevada and "downtown" Vegas the rule is altered somewhat, requiring the dealer to hit a soft 17. It's a nasty ploy, and definitely a disadvantage to the player.

On the table layout in "strip" casinos, it clearly states, "the dealer must stand on *all* 17's." Much better!

If you are inexperienced, or not an active player, I recommend that you review the previous pages before we go on to basic strategy. Be sure you fully understand the basic game, and particularly the player options: hit, stand, split, double down, and surrender.

CHAPTER 3

BASIC STRATEGY

Before we look at the charts, let's apply some good old-fashioned "horse-sense" and see if we can understand the reasoning behind them. You'll be able to remember the strategies so much easier if you understand why they work!

STIFF AND PAT HANDS

First, let's identify the potential "bust" hands as "stiffs." And it's a great term for them. When the dealer gives you a 12, 13, 14, 15, or 16, you got "stiffed!" If your hand is 15 or 16, you've got one of the two worst hands possible, and especially tough if the dealer's up-card is a 7 or higher.

Don't screw it up anymore than it already is by *not* hitting it, or *not* surrendering it if you can.

If your cards total 17, 18, 19, or 20, it's a "pat" hand. It's decent. Although 17 and 18 may be good enough to stand on, they certainly won't get all the "marbles" all the time. 19's, 20's, and Blackjack's are the real "goodies" you're looking for.

PLAYER DRAWS FIRST

Judging by what we now understand to be the object of the game, and the basic game rules themselves, it would appear that the biggest casino advantage is the fact that the player has to draw *before* the dealer does.

That simple fact accounts for a hefty 7% advantage to the house.* So many inexperienced players sensing that problem, elect to never hit a stiff for fear of busting. That dumb little ploy is worth about 3% to the house. We can work down the 7% advantage other ways, but not *that* way!

---

*Since all casinos pay 3 to 2 for a Blackjack, this effectively lowers the 7% house advantage to a little less than 5%.

Player options based on "basic strategy," including hitting, standing, doubling, and splitting for both hard and soft hands will lower the house percentage to about ½%. This number cannot be determined precisely because of variations in rules from one casino to another, and the frequent rule changes

GOOD CARDS AND BAD CARDS

Now, see if you can identify the "good" cards and the "bad" cards for the player. It's important. Think about it.

It would seem obvious that all 10-cards are good, because they help give you 20's, and pair-up nicely with an ace for a Blackjack. Sure, **10-cards are good!**

What about 2's, 3's, 4's, 5's, and 6's? They help to promote those lousy stiffs, right? And more importantly, they can improve a dealer's stiff hand without necessarily busting. **2's, 3's, 4's, 5's, and 6's are indeed, bad cards!**

Although we're getting a little ahead of ourselves, the object of *counting* is to determine how many 10-value cards and how many 2's, 3's, 4's, 5's, and 6's are *left in the deck,* based on how many you've seen *come out of the deck.*

When the ratio of 10-cards to "little cards" is high, the player has an advantage. If there are too many little cards left in the deck, the dealer has a distinct advantage.

that occur. In addition, a multiple-deck game will add at least ½% to the casino's edge, regardless of the player's counting technique.

Mediocre strategy may give the casino another 2-3% advantage. A poor strategy may increase the casino's edge to 5% or more!

BASIC STRATEGY DEPENDS ON THE DEALER'S UP-CARD

As you read the charts coming up, you'll notice that our strategy depends on *both* our hand total and the dealer's up-card.

Multiple-deck games will affect our percentages and the strategies that follow, but only to a limited degree. However, it can be concluded that multiple-deck games are indeed an advantage to the dealer, not to the player!

HIT OR STAND STRATEGY FOR STIFFS

PLAYER'S HARD HAND	DEALER'S UP-CARD									
	2	3	4	5	6	7	8	9	10	A
16										
15										
14	S	T	A	N	D		H	I	T	
13										
12	H	IT								

ALWAYS STAND ON 17 OR BETTER!

Our strategy for hitting or standing with stiffs is really quite simple as you can see.

Always hit a stiff when the dealer has a 7 or higher. Remember it as 7-UP, and you'll never forget it.

Always stand on a stiff when the dealer has a 6 or less showing, with the exception of 12. The dealer does not have a pat hand (with the exception of ace-6) so there is a good possibility the dealer will bust.

Always stand on 17 or better. Never, even in your wildest dreams hit 17! Dealers must alert pit bosses in many casinos when a player hits 17 or better. See if you can guess why.

Always draw a card on 11 or less. You might actually double down or split depending on the card values, but at the very least, you'll always hit it.

Incidentally, the hit and stand rules apply not only to your original hand, *but to your hand at any time.* For example, if your original hand is 10-4 against the dealer's 10, you hit it. You receive a 2. Now you have 16. According to the chart, you must continue hitting (until you have 17 or better).

Sure, the odds are against you, but you had a losing hand in the first place. Over the long term, you'll reduce the casino's initial advantage we talked about by about 2½% with correct hitting and standing strategy. Reducing the percentages against you is the name of the game.

HARD DOUBLE DOWN STRATEGY

PLAYER'S HARD HAND	DEALER'S UP-CARD									
	2	3	4	5	6	7	8	9	10	A
11			D	O	U	B	L	E		
10				D	O	W	N			
9							H	I	T	

Notice that the player should **always double down on 11,** regardless of the dealer's up-card.

Doubling on 10 is restricted to a dealer's up-card of 9 or lower. If the dealer's up-card is 10 or an ace, it's obviously too risky.

Some experts differ on the rule for 9, ironically. Our position must be to **only double down on 9 if the dealer's up-card is 3, 4, 5, or 6.**

It's a mute point in many casinos (especially Northern Nevada) where doubling is limited to 10 or 11. Doubling after you have split is equally restricted in many casinos. Ask before you play to be sure you understand the rules in a particular casino. **Always seek out the best playing conditions.**

Proper strategy for hard double downs (and for soft doubling that we'll cover under "Soft Hand Strategy") further reduces the casino percentage by about 1½%. We're getting there!

SPLITTING STRATEGY

PLAYER'S HAND	DEALER'S UP-CARD									
	2	3	4	5	6	7	8	9	10	A
A-A			S	P	L	I	T			
10-10			S	T	A	N	D			
9-9										
8-8			S	P	L	I	T			
7-7										
6-6							H	I	T	
5-5		D	O	U	B	L	E			
4-4							H	I	T	
3-3			S	PL	I	T				
2-2										

Most computer-aided strategies for splitting pairs are randomly defined, with no symmetry to recognize. It's exceedingly difficult for the layman player to remember. In fact, most player-errors in basic strategy are made when splitting.

Accordingly, I've taken the liberty of simplifying our splitting strategy to make it much easier to remember, with only a minuscule trade-off in accuracy.

Since the overall advantage to the player for correct splitting is less than ½% (the smallest of all the player options) there's no reason to be alarmed. The simplification of an otherwise complex strategy is justifiably appropriate for this text.

Here's how to remember our special splitting strategy:

Always split aces and 8's. Never split 10's, 5's and 4's.

Treat 5-5 as 10 and follow our double down rule —double if the dealer shows 9 or less, otherwise just hit.

Split 9's when the dealer has 9 or less, split 7's when the dealer has 7 or less, and split 6's when the dealer has 6 or less. Remember that the dealer's up-card is always the same or less than the card you're splitting with 6's, 7's, and 9's.

Only split 3's and 2's when the dealer's up-card is 4, 5, 6, or 7. Otherwise just hit.

SOFT HAND STRATEGY

PLAYER'S SOFT HAND	DEALER'S UP-CARD									
	2	3	4	5	6	7	8	9	10	A
A-9 (20)			S	T	A	N	D			
A-8 (19)										
A-7 (18)				D						
A-6 (17)				O						
A-5 (16)	H			U						
A-4 (15)	I			B			H	I	T	
A-3 (14)	T			L						
A-2 (13)				E						

Once again, our "soft" strategy has been ever-so-slightly simplified to make it easier for you to remember.

Always stand on a soft 19 and 20. They represent good hands regardless of the dealer's up-card.

Always double down (if it's allowed) on a soft 13 through 18 when the dealer has a 4, 5, or 6 showing. Otherwise hit 13 through 17.

A soft 18 is the most difficult to remember because there are three options. **Always double down on a soft 18 when the dealer is showing a 4, 5, or 6 (just like the smaller soft hands) and hit it when the dealer is showing a 9, 10, or ace.**

With a 9 or higher up-card, the dealer may have

a better hand, so it does pay to try to improve your soft 18. Remember, you can't bust any soft hand with a single hit. However, if you end up with a poor draw, such as a 5, you must hit it again (hard 13) and take your chances.

SURRENDER STRATEGY

The rules for surrender are so simple, we don't need a chart to show you.

PLAYER'S HAND	DEALER'S UP-CARD
15-16 (hard)	7-8-9-10-A

Many gaming experts disagree on surrendering a 15 or 16 to the dealer's 7 or 8 up-card. Most all agree to surrender on a 9, 10, or ace up.

This is *my* book, so I'm telling you *my way* to do it. **Surrender a 15 or 16 stiff (except 8-8) when the dealer has a 7 or higher up-card,** *if you're playing in a casino where they allow it.* You should be.

And wouldn't you know it, the casinos can't agree on surrender rules either. Some allow you to surrender your hand only after the dealer has checked a 10 or ace up-card for Blackjack. A few other casinos, very few, will allow the surrender before the hole-card is checked. It's worth nearly 1% to you. So look for it. Don't hesitate to lose half of your bet with a bad hand. It beats losing it all!

PRACTICE YOUR "SKILL"

Now that we have presented a solid, basic strategy, it's important that you memorize the charts, so you'll know exactly what to do with every conceivable hand and dealer up-card.

The instant you see your cards, make your decision right away! Don't guess. Follow basic strategy exactly! There's no reason to ponder.

Find a deck around the house and practice! *Don't bet a dollar until you've mastered the strategy.*

Like anything else, our basic strategy charts will at first appear too complicated to memorize. But as you dig into it, and practice, your "skill" should become second nature. Yes, your effectiveness can only be measured by how much you practice. I'm sure it took Terry Bradshaw a long time to learn how to throw a football. And how long do you suppose Earl Anthony practiced throwing strikes? I know, this isn't football or bowling, but it *is* a game! How well you are prepared will have a direct and lasting effect on your confidence level. And you know how important that is! Make a decision right now whether or not you'll be able to do it. **You must have confidence in yourself before you can have any confidence in your game.**

THE ADVANTAGE OF BASIC STRATEGY

What advantage does the casino have against a player with good, basic strategy? I was hoping you wouldn't ask me that question! Every gaming expert in the world has tried to come up with a nifty number. But no one can pin-point it.

Even with today's advanced, high-speed, powerful computers, no one can give you a precise casino advantage because of the rule extremes that vary significantly from one casino to another.

Is the game one-deck or a multiple-shoe?

Does the dealer stand on all 17's or hit a soft 17?

Can I double down on any two cards, or is it limited to 10 or 11?

Can I double after I split?

Can I resplit aces?

Is surrender available?

Can I surrender before the dealer checks his hole-card?

And as I've mentioned before, even if you know the game rules in a particular casino, they may change tomorrow. Totally unstable!

The Player's Accuracy

Suppose we could find an exact percentage based on a certain set of rules, and we could if we wanted to. Now what?

Do you play a basic strategy absolutely perfect? I doubt it. Are you mediocre? Probably. If you're a poor player, you'll give back most of the casino's 5% advantage or more.

Do you see the point? No player is infallible. To what degree do we correctly apply basic strategy? It's a significant question in determining the casino's edge.

The Advantage is Based on Long-Term Decisions

Still another matter that you must consider when weighing the casino's percentage is the fact that it's built on long-term decisions. Nothing says the percentages can't vary 10% or more during the short term! There are incredible fluctuations that can occur, especially with a single-deck game.

Hopefully, all the big fluctuations will fall in your favor, but don't be so naive as to think you can't lose ten hands in a row. You can, and you will . . . sometime. There are no guarantees over the *short term*. You must understand this!

An arbitrary percentage of 1% (an acceptable number) only tells us that over a *very long period*, we will probably lose $1 for every $100 we bet. It would theoretically take 10,000 plays for the casino to take all our money, betting $1 a hand. So you can see the 1%, although a very small number, will wipe you out, eventually. Don't be misled by little numbers!

Basic Strategy Makes the Game About Even

I like to consider the casino advantage of ½% based on average playing conditions for an average player using basic strategy. My number is about as useless as any other expert's number, because of all the reasons we've just cited.

Of course, if an "exceptional" player has found a casino with "exceptional" game rules, blackjack can be considered "even." With surrender, the player may actually have a slight edge.

I got a big kick out of a leading expert's number for the casino percentage. He made a big deal out of it as if the "media" should report on his findings!

Not to embarrass him, I'll change it a little but keep the same number of digits. That's the ridiculous part. He says blackjack with basic strategy is .347%!

There's no qualification as to the particular game rules, and why carry it out to three places? It's a totally useless, meaningless number, unless you plan on playing literally tens of thousands of hands under optimum playing conditions without a single error in strategy.

What we *can* determine from our analysis however, is that blackjack is about as safe to play as craps. I'm not saying it's safe, I'm saying it's about the same. Using basic strategy (with 95% accuracy) and under "decent" playing conditions, I rate both games a toss-up.

However, if a player goes one step further and masters a count strategy to identify the fluctuations while they're occuring, blackjack is indeed a better game. Knowing to increase your bet size when the opportunity is there, and laying back when the opportunity is gone, is the tremendous advantage to keeping track of the cards.

Keeping track of the *dice* is a waste of time. Previous rolls have no effect on future rolls. But at the blackjack table, previous cards *do indeed* have an effect on future cards.

On to the next chapter. Counting!

CHAPTER 4

COUNTING THE CARDS

Most gaming experts who have authored other books, steadfastly believe that you must keep a running track of all cards that have been dealt, follow an ever-changing basic strategy, and then adjust your betting for that rare moment (about 5% of the time) when the odds have shifted in your favor. In a nutshell, that's the computer-proven, mathematical approach to beating the game.

In order to keep an accurate "count" of the dealt cards, you must be able to concentrate fully. The casino won't let you drag in a portable computer terminal. Even a pencil and pad of paper are a no-no. To use the popular "count" systems widely advertised today, you simply must have a good memory recall, and the stamina to stay with it.

If you can't keep the count as you're suppose to, and you flat-out refuse to learn "basic strategy," then blackjack will end up about a 5% game for the house, or better!

I'm not trying to scare you away. I'm just giving it to you like it is. You see, blackjack is a unique game that requires two special skills. You already know about one of them—basic strategy. The other is counting. The professional player who might actually have a long-term advantage over the casino is a master at both.

Unfortunately, a high-level counting strategy, fully detailed, is far beyond the scope of this text. None-the-less, I'm going to give you the raw basics of a powerful counting system later on, for when you might be ready for it. At least you won't have to go out and buy another book!

For now, in order to realize at least something from the counting concept, I'll show you a way to take a "little" advantage from it. A way that's remarkably easy. But it's a compromise. And yes, there will be some work to do. Practicing your "second" skill will be important, and hopefully a "fun" experience for you.

HISTORY OF COUNTING

Many players today presume that keeping track of the cards is a relatively new concept. Surprisingly, the first count strategy was developed over twenty years ago in 1963, by Dr. Edward O. Thorp, and widely publicized in his famous book, *Beat the Dealer.* Thorp based his revolutionary concept on work performed nearly ten years earlier by Roger Baldwin and a team of researchers.

Baldwin developed a basic strategy for player options, much as we know it today. Thorp devised a system for counting 10-value cards, working in conjunction with Julian H. Braun, a computer expert at IBM. Braun became active in blackjack analysis on his own, and made significant individual contributions.

The original work of these principal founders has seen little refinement over the years. A testimony to the accuracy of their work. Baldwin, Thorp, and Braun deserve the lion's share of the credit for pioneering count systems and basic strategy.

Today, there are literally hundreds of blackjack systems available, some at ridiculously high prices, but all based on the original work of this elite group.

THE BASIS OF COUNTING

We've already hinted to you what counting is and why it works. In essence, we know that little cards help the dealer, and larger cards help the player. Based on that critical aspect, it would logically follow that you must keep track of the little cards and the big cards as they appear, and ascertain the remaining cards in the deck by simple subtraction.

Thorp's original 10-count system was never seriously challenged for accuracy. Indeed, who would be dumb enough to challenge a computer! The problem however, arose immediately. It was too complicated for the layman player to use! Thorp recommended a computation of 10-cards and little cards in the form of a ratio. The computation had to be done in the player's head. No easy matter.

THE POINT-COUNT

Finally, a balanced system of counting was devised whereby a "minus" number is assigned to a large card, and a "plus" number assigned to a small card. Forgetting the ratios, the player would simply count the plus numbers and the minus numbers to determine the deck construction at any moment.

Today, the systems that are plus and minus numbers are commonly called "point-count" systems and are generally regarded as the most powerful.

A Typical Point-Count System

PLUS (COUNT +1)					MINUS (COUNT −1)				
2	3	4	5	6	7	8	9	10	A
1	1	1	1	1	0	0	0	1	1

To actually use this counting strategy, the player literally counts the cards as they appear from the shoe (or hand), counting "+1" for the little cards and "−1" for the big ones. Only the 10-value cards and the ace are worth counting as plus values in this case; the middle values, 7, 8, and 9, are incidental and not worth tracking.

You can now see why card counters demand a "cards-up" game. It's much easier to count them! When the cards are dealt face-down, the counter must wait until a player busts to see those particular cards, or until the other players settle their wagers. It's also the reason why sharp counters always want to play at "third base." That's the last position at the table—to the player's far left, and allows the counter to see more cards exposed before he must act on his hand.

COUNTING HAS TWO ADVANTAGES

The advantage to counting is two-fold. For one, *the counter will adjust the size of his bet as the count changes.* When the count is a high plus-value, he will increase his bet-size because many small cards have been removed from the deck, out of ratio to the normal distribution. Similarly, when the count he is mentally keeping turns to a low negative-value, he will greatly reduce his bet, or perhaps wait out the shuffle—maybe leave the table entirely. He has a "negative expectancy" so why play?

The other advantage to counting is *the player's ability to change basic strategy as the count* changes. For example, if the counter knows an unusually large number of 10-value cards are out of the deck, he may decide not to double down, even though he has an 11-value hand and would certainly double on it under normal circumstances.

In fact, a professional counter follows an ever-changing basic strategy as his count continually fluctuates. He has memorized and recalls data from at least five or six different strategies for all the player options; computes the new count as each card appears; adjusts his bets in relation to this count; watches out for the pit bosses; and tunes-out all other distractions of the casino.

Holy Toledo!

You're right if you think this takes the fun out of the game for the great majority of players. You can expect a mild headache. But it's the counter's way of work. For them, it's serious business.

When I'm playing, I use a count strategy called the "Imperial Count" that I devised a few years ago and detailed in *Pay the Line*. Although that particular count scheme differs vastly from the point-count I've just revealed, and is considerably easier to master, it too is beyond the scope of a beginner's book.

COUNTING IS TOO IMPORTANT FOR EVEN A BEGINNER TO IGNORE

The mention of counting here was a difficult decision for me to make. I decided that if the book is about blackjack, and is going to be more complete than the other cursory beginner books I've seen, at least an introduction to counting had to be included, whether it's grade-school or college-level. At the very least, my readers would understand what counting is about, and why it's done, regardless of whether it's journalistically right or wrong to include in a beginner's text.

Besides, I mentioned earlier that I would tell beginners how to achieve at least some advantage to the counting concept without making the all-out effort. Now's the time.

A COUNTING "OVER-VIEW"

Without counting, the best a player can do is master basic strategy for the player options, and shop the casinos for the best game rules. With surrender, it's possible to conclude that the player can find a *nearly* "even" game* (which isn't bad) but

*½ to 1½% casino advantage.

the temptation to take it one step further without complications, is the next logical progression in skill.

COUNT WITHOUT ACTUALLY COUNTING

Here's how you can use counting, without actually counting!

In my own studies, I've determined that a good counting skill is the most useful when the ratio of little cards to big cards is dramatically off kelter. Obviously, that's the time to really act. You might bet a little heavier, or you might leave the table, depending on whether the deviation is good or bad for the player.

Start out by just tracking the little cards—2, 3, 4, 5, and 6. *On average, two of every five cards should be a little one.* If you see ten cards on the table, four of them should be small. If it turns out that six or seven of them are small, you have an edge *at that moment*. If only one or two cards are small, the dealer retains the advantage.

Surprisingly, when such fluctuations occur in a large degree, it will appear almost obvious to the player who is *only aware of what to look for, without actually keeping the count.* This practice is what I call a counting "over-view." Most all dealers are trained to look for it, and so are the pit bosses, especially at "downtown" casinos or wherever single decks are in play.

An Actual Experience Using Over-View

The best example of a counting over-view happened to me February 1985 at the Desert Inn, Las Vegas. The "DI" deals a six-deck shoe, not much of a treat for card counters as I'll explain later. In any event, I played a dealer head-on (no other players at the table) and noticed the first few hands were all 5's, 6's, a few 4's, 7's and 8's . . . not a single face-card! After ten or so hands, all but a few of the 24 5-value cards had been dealt! The odds of that happening are staggering! Since a 5-value card is the worst for the player of all the little cards, it gave me a tremendous advantage for the rest of the shoe. The 5's were nearly all gone! How could anyone not have noticed!

Eventually, the shoe began to "right" itself somewhat, and I ended up winning only a token amount. I'm telling you this because there's a big lesson in it. Even under superbly ideal conditions, there was no guarantee, for me or for anyone. Sure, I won, but it turned out to be less than the expectancy. Anything can happen in short-term play!

The important thing here is my awareness of the swing in expectancy from negative to positive. Now, you can be aware of it too . . . and use it to your advantage!

HOW TO BET USING OVER-VIEW

Press up your winning bets, up to but not more than three times, when the little cards seem to be

out in abundance; lay back, or walk away when the 10's and ace's seem exhausted.

A chart of detailed betting levels would not be appropriate here, since for simplicity sake, there is no detail to the counting strategy. However, most casinos with one or two decks, and a haven for counters, will generally shuffle the deck *at any time* when a player suddenly increases his bet size by more than three times.

The Fremont Shuffle

One of my favorite playgrounds is the pit of single-deck tables at the Fremont Hotel, in downtown Las Vegas. I know most of the dealers, and unfortunately, they know me! They'll shuffle whenever I raise my bet four times! They know I'm counting, and assume that I know what I'm doing.

I can recall the time I tested the dealer by increasing my bet five times when the count was bad! I thought I'd get a fresh shuffle. As it turned out, the hand played! The dealer must have been counting also!

Incidentally, the Fremont offers "surrender." The playing conditions are ideal. But don't count on it lasting forever. Casinos change their rules frequently.

Small Cards Control Your Betting Level

My recommendation is that you increase your winning bets to the degree that you see a relative number of small cards in bunches, or favorably out of ratio to the remaining deck. A modest player advantage might signal a bet that's 50% more than your previous winning wager. That's all. And even though I'm counting, I make it a point *not to press* a losing wager.

For most players, you'll be able to read a table's complexion after a few hours of playing time. Better yet, after a few hours of practicing at home! You'll get a pretty good idea of the remaining deck construction simply by a review of the dealt cards, noting any unusual excess or deficiency in small cards.

SINGLE-DECK VS. THE SHOE

Large fluctuations occur rarely. Most of the time, the deck runs fairly normal in the way the little cards and big cards are arranged. The likelihood of a large fluctuation, good or bad, is greater in single and two-deck games, as opposed to the 6-deck and 8-deck shoes. That's why most counters prefer a single deck. Can you appreciate that the large quantity of cards in the multiple-deck shoe tend to thin out the fluctuations? And even if we've found a big swing in the ratio, the remaining cards in the multiple-deck will throw off our expectancy. More so, a multiple-deck is difficult to count. For the beginner, it's not going to be that significant whether you're playing a single deck or shoe table. But as you progress in experience, look for the few single-deck games that remain, and watch for the fluctuations that can occur.

A COMPARISON OF PLAYING CONDITIONS IN ATLANTIC CITY AND NEVADA

If you look for a single-deck game in Atlantic City, you might as well look for the Himalayas. As of this writing, mostly 6-deck and 8-deck games prevail. One casino is dealing a few 4-deck games; that's the best you can do!

Although the New Jersey Casino Control Commission requires that game rules are uniformly the same among casinos, the number of decks is not considered a "rule." However, the commission does require that all cards are dealt from a shoe, not by hand. Supposedly, any casino could install a one-deck shoe. The common excuse is that it would cut down on the number of decisions per hour.

Atlantic City casinos have a wide base of customers. So many, in fact, that they really don't need a single-deck game to lure players. They already have them.

In 1981, the Casino Control Commission obliged the casinos in their petition to prohibit "surrender" entirely. The casinos claimed they were losing too much money! Chuckle, chuckle.

Incidentally, the regulatory agency also prohibits sports-betting, poker, and keno.

Don't look for much improvement in playing conditions out East until there's less regulation and more casinos. In Nevada, there's no stymie to competition since the casinos are pretty much free to set the game rules as they please. Plus, there's a lot of casinos, drawing from a smaller market of players.

Good, healthy competition in any marketplace, free of regulation, invariably benefits the customer. Accordingly, you'll find that most of the real professional gamblers play in Nevada. They know where the best rules are.

CHAPTER 5

HOW TO BET

The subject of betting—all kinds of progressions and theories, has been known to fill entire books!

Some authors recommend that you press up your bets when you're losing, to recoup the losses, based on the dangerous idea that you can't possibly lose ten hands in a row. You can. And you will, sometime. Never press up during a losing session!

BETTING PROGRESSIONS

If you happen to get hooked on gambling books, I'm sure you'll run across many betting progressions such as 1-2-3-1-2. The first bet is a single unit, then two-units, etc. All these betting progressions are pure foolishness! **In any random game, with a negative expectancy, it makes absolutely no difference over the long term how you vary the size of your bets.** If the casino has a built-in house advantage, it will always prove out, eventually.

It shoots down a lot of interesting theories, but what I've just told you is impeccably true. *You can't change a negative expectancy into a positive expectancy by the way you bet.* Believe it!

But wait a minute! Blackjack has a continually changing expectancy, remember? However, only the few players keeping track of the cards can identify it, and adjust their bets accordingly. If you're not keeping track, then there's little point in varying your bet size.

A COMMON RULE OF BETTING

This is a good place to mention a popular betting recommendation that appears to clash somewhat with our betting rule of maintaining a constant level for non-counters. *Press up when you're winning, and lay back or quit when you're losing.*

On the surface, it seems to make good sense, and it appears to be safe, conservative advice. By pressing up when you're ahead, you're betting back some of your winnings, instead of your hard-earned stake, and have actually progressed to a higher betting level without putting yourself in jeopardy. If you're at the right table, at the right time, this advice makes darn good sense!

The only real advantage to pressing up during a win-streak is to insure that you don't miss out on it. But then again, how do you know when it's coming?

The recommendation to lay back or quit when you're losing makes good sense too, right? Indeed it does.

But remember our important rule. *Over the long term,* it makes no difference how you vary your betting, unless you're counting the cards.

BET SAFELY

Above all, **never make a bet that you can't afford to lose, or that makes you uncomfortable.** While at the dice tables at the MGM Las Vegas recently, I complained to a pit boss that the dice weren't passing. He was a friend of mine so I kidded him a little about how cold the table was, and how much money the casino was making. He said, "Oh, maybe you don't understand, John . . . at midnight, we give all our winnings back to the players, and you have to give back any money that you won too."

Right!

Never lose track of the fact that you're playing with real money.

And they won't give it back!

Your First Bet

For most beginning players, I strongly recommend that you begin playing for the first time at a $1 table, if you find it. In Las Vegas, try the downtown casinos. On the strip, look for a $2 minimum table. Reno has lots of $1 tables except at the MGM where $2 tables are plentiful. In Atlantic City, $5 and $10 tables are widely in use.

The table minimums are clearly posted on color-coded signs mounted directly on the table. Casinos usually follow the same color-code as their chips. White represents a $1 or $2 minimum. Red is for $5, green is $25, and black means $100. The maximum bets that are allowed vary widely from one casino to another. Generally, $2,000 is the maximum in most casinos, if that's of any significance to you.

Finding the Right Table Minimum

The casinos make it difficult for the small bettor to find a $2 minimum table on weekend evenings. I wonder why.

As soon as the casino starts getting busy, all of a sudden the $2 tables become $5 tables, and $5 tables become $25 tables. As in any other business, the casinos know all about "supply and demand."

Don't be forced into playing at a table that requires a larger minimum bet than you want to make. Be disciplined! Try to avoid the weekends if possible, or get up early and try it in the early morning hours. It's a much better time to play. There's less competition among players for the $2 tables, and a more relaxing atmosphere. Besides, chances are you're sharper in the morning, awake and ready to go. Mornings are the only time I play, for all these reasons. Try it!

TIPPING AT THE TABLES

In my first book, *Pay the Line,* I recommended that you only tip the dealer *at the end of a playing session,* not during play.

A lot of readers asked, "why wait?" suggesting that if you tip during a good win streak, the dealer will be cheering for you, and hopefully sharing in your profits. It's possible, some readers thought, that a dealer might actually help you win! (Knowing that you are a good tipper.)

And that's precisely the reason why you should not tip while you're playing! Here's an example that should make the point clear.

Dealer Exposes Hole-card

At the Desert Inn, a few years ago, I sat into a situation at the blackjack tables that probably only happens once in a million hands. A new dealer, as evidenced by her slow, indecisive play and occasional mistakes, had not been properly trained in how to hide her hole-card. My position at the table was "first base," chosen purely at random, but the best spot to see a hole card, if the dealer is particularly sloppy.

As you know, in most casinos the dealer always checks her hole-card when a 10-value or ace is up, to determine if she has a blackjack before the players act on their hands.

To my surprise, everytime this new girl checked her hole-card, she showed it to me. She might as well have stuck the card in my face! It was that blatant. I played a few hands, wondering what the hell to do; continue taking advantage of this incredible situation, move away and avoid the possible confrontation, or tell the pit boss about it. Other players at the table were getting suspicious.

You see, in the great majority of times that a casino is being cheated (especially with a shoe game), it's based on a collusion between a dealer and a player; the dealer in some way clues the player as to a hole-card value. Eye motions, twitches, arm or finger movement. A coded program to get the answer to the player.

Now put yourself in my position. What if a pit boss noticed that the dealer was showing me her hole-card? No doubt the boss would notice that I was winning significantly and tipping the dealer. Do you see that the boss might have thought I had a scam going against the casino, working with the dealer?

Forget it! I don't want to be escorted by a security agent into their interrogation room, and possibly arrested. A little publicity never hurts a gaming author, but not that kind!

I elected to leave the table and later told a pit boss about the condition. I watched him correct the dealer's mistake. He looked over to me and thanked me for calling it to his attention. That table could have lost thousands and any player taking advantage of it, could have been in serious trouble!

Will The Dealer "Help" You Win?

Tipping a dealer during play, probably does not encourage any "help" on the dealer's part, but it's possible. The casino's concern is that if very large tips are to be "played" by the dealer, along with the player's bet, it's a temptation they want no part of.

For example, a friend of mine who plays regularly, claims that he can influence the dealer's aid by making large tips. He said that at one time, with large tips out for the dealer, a decision to hit or stand on a stiff would be indicated by the dealer's actions—moving rapidly past the player if the dealer had a potential "bust" hand, or stopping at the player's position and just waiting, a telling signal that the dealer had a "pat" hand.

If you are ever accused of working illegally with a dealer, even though you aren't, the casino won't drag you out in the desert and break your knees. But you might be arrested, if the casino thinks they have a case. At the least, you will be detained, and embarrassed.

For these reasons, I never make a bet for the dealer during play, or tip them at all until the session is over . . . and I'm gone.

I'll tell you about making these bets for the dealers, even though I don't recommend it, so that you know how it works.

Any bet inside the player's betting circle is the player's money, as far as the casino is concerned. Any bet outside the circle and towards the dealer is the dealer's bet. If the hand wins, the dealer's bet is paid off and removed from the table. It can't "ride." Again, for the reasons that the casino doesn't want the dealer to be financially involved with the game to any significant levels.

If the dealer's bet is *inside* the betting circle, then the bet can ride, because the casino considers that bet the property of the player, not of the dealer. It's up to the player to give it to the dealer, at any time, if he so decides.

To be safe, do as I do, tip the dealer only at the end of a playing session, and only if the dealer has been friendly and courteous. Don't tip a rude dealer, regardless of your successes, no more than you would tip a rude, arrogant waitress in a restaurant.

The Casino Hustle

In a recent interview with Scott Zamost, casino editor with the Las Vegas Sun, Zamost asked, "What bothers you the most in casinos?" My response to him was the annoying hustling that sometimes goes on especially from the craps dealers, who beckon the players to make a bet "for the boys." I have an aversion to being hustled, and will leave that table at once. I suggest you do the same. The question was in vogue at the time of the interview as I understand an entire dice crew had been fired from a big strip hotel for hustling the players.

At a dice table recently, my wife was playing with several other women at the table and winning. The dice were really passing. During play, the stickman told the girls, "Hey, how about making a bet for *us*, we're not just here for your fun!"

On that demand, a few girls did indeed make a bet for the dealers, and my wife gave them dirty looks, and left. I wish I had been there. I would have read them the riot act!

This does happen. The player must understand that the dealers are indeed there for the player's fun. It's a sad commentary.

CHAPTER 6

THINGS YOU MUST DO

1. CONDITION YOURSELF IN A WINNING FRAME OF MIND. Think positive!
2. DEVELOP CONFIDENCE IN YOUR ABILITY. Learn the game rules fully, and be sure you have mastered basic strategy before you play. Here are a few highlights:
   (1) Never take insurance.
   (2) Always stand on 17 or better.
   (3) Always hit 12 through 16 against a dealer's 7 or higher.

    (4) Never hit 12 through 16 against a dealer's 6 or less (except 12 against a 2 or 3).

    (5) Always double down on 11.

    (6) Always double down on 10 against a 9 or less.

    (7) Always split aces and 8's.

    (8) Never split 5's or 10's.

3. SEEK OUT THE BEST PLAYING CONDITIONS. For example:

    (1) Double down on any two cards.

    (2) Double down after you split.

    (3) Dealer stands on all 17's.

    (4) Surrender is offered.

    (5) Cards are dealt face-up (for counting).

    (6) One or two-decks are in play (for counting).

4. PLAY AT YOUR OWN PACE. Don't let a dealer or other player rush or upset you. If anything at the table bothers you, leave at once.

5. BET SAFELY. Don't make any bet that you can't afford to lose. Always begin with a relatively small wager.

6. PRESS UP WHEN YOU'RE WINNING, LAY BACK OR QUIT WHEN YOU'RE LOSING. This way, you're increasing your chances to win larger bets by using some of your winnings against the casino. But be careful. The casino is no place for a reckless spender.

7. NEVER PRESS WHEN YOU'RE LOSING. If losses persist. Quit!

8. SET A LIMIT ON YOUR LOSSES. If you reach it, quit!

9. LEARN HOW TO QUIT WINNERS! If you're up substantially at any time during a session, set aside some winnings to insure the win.

10. BE SATISFIED WITH A WIN OF ANY AMOUNT. If you're greedy, and have no concept of quitting, you're a loser even before you begin.

11. NEVER PLAY WHEN YOU'RE TIRED. Only when you're sharp, alert, and relaxed.

12. TRY COUNTING THE CARDS. Even if you're a beginner, there's no reason you can't try the over-view strategy covered in this text. It's easy!

13. PLAY ONLY DURING THE MORNING OR EARLY AFTERNOON WHEN THE CASINO IS NOT BUSY. Avoid weekends, especially weekend evenings when the casino is too crowded. It might be hard to find a seat at a low minimum table.

14. Although it's not a "must," it's nice to tip the dealer *at the end of your session,* not during play, if you've won substantially *and* if the dealer was polite and courteous. A rude dealer (and the casino) only deserves the absence of your play.

Good luck!